I've heard it said that
"You should never pass up
a chance to let someone know
how much they mean to you."

And as soon as I saw this,
I knew that I had a wonderful
way to let you know
how special you are...
to me.

Blue Mountain Arts®
Bestselling Books

By Susan Polis Schutz:
To My Daughter, with Love, on the Important Things in Life
To My Son, with Love
I Love You

Is It Time to Make a Change?
by Deanna Beisser

To the Love of My Life
by Donna Fargo

100 Things to Always Remember... and One Thing to Never Forget
Chasing Away the Clouds
For You, Just Because You're Very Special to Me
To the One Person I Consider to Be My Soul Mate
by Douglas Pagels

Being a Teen ...Words of Advice from Someone Who's Been There
by Diane Mastromarino

girls rule ...a very special book created especially for girls
by Ashley Rice

A Lifetime of Love ...Poems on the Passages of Life
by Leonard Nimoy

Anthologies:
42 Gifts I'd Like to Give to You
Always Believe in Yourself and Your Dreams
A Daughter Is Forever
For You, My Daughter
Friends for Life
I Love You, Mom
I'm Glad You Are My Sister
The Joys and Challenges of Motherhood
The Language of Recovery ...and Living Life One Day at a Time
Life Can Be Hard Sometimes ...but It's Going to Be Okay
May You Always Have an Angel by Your Side
Take Each Day One Step at a Time
Teaching and Learning Are Lifelong Journeys
There Is Greatness Within You, My Son
These Are the Gifts I'd Like to Give to You
Think Positive Thoughts Every Day
Thoughts to Share with a Wonderful Teenager
To My Child
With God by Your Side ...You Never Have to Be Alone

I Want You to Read This Today and Remember It Forever

———— ⇌ ————

Thoughts to share with a very special person

by Douglas Pagels

Blue Mountain Press™

SPS Studios, Inc., Boulder, Colorado

Library of Congress Control Number: 2002093604
ISBN: 0-88396-680-8

Certain trademarks are used under license.

Manufactured in China.
First Printing: 2003

 This book is printed on recycled paper.

This book is printed on fine quality, laid embossed, 80 lb. paper. This paper has been specially produced to be acid free (neutral pH) and contains no groundwood or unbleached pulp. It conforms with all the requirements of the American National Standards Institute, Inc., so as to ensure that this book will last and be enjoyed by future generations.

SPS Studios, Inc.
P.O. Box 4549, Boulder, Colorado 80306

CONTENTS

I Wish for You

Happiness. Deep down within.
Serenity. With each sunrise.
Success. In each facet of your life.
Close and caring friends.
Love. That never ends.

Special memories. Of all
    the yesterdays.
A bright today. With so much
    to be thankful for.
A path. That leads to
    beautiful tomorrows.

Dreams. That do their best to come true.
And appreciation. Of all the wonderful
        things about you.

I Want You to Read This Today...
and Remember It
Forever

If I could only share one heartfelt thought
with one person
for all the rest of my days,
you would be that person
and this would be
   the message...

With the deepest kind of gratitude and the
sweetest kind of joy, I simply want to thank
you for being
      all that you are to me...

You are truly amazing. Don't let anyone ever tell you otherwise. You are a treasure a million times more valuable than the ones some people spend a lifetime trying to find. You are a one-of-a-kind inspiration, someone whom anyone would be privileged to know. And I am as proud as I can be... to know you as well as I do.

So please... accept this special thanks and remember it in all the days ahead, whether time finds us far apart or it keeps us close together.

I want you to remember these words today...
and all the rest
of forever.

————— ⌒ —————

I have something to tell you. It's a
little hard to describe with words, but
I know that if *anyone* will understand
what I'm trying to say... you will.

The things that warm a person's
heart, that fill a person's soul, and
that make it hard to count one's
blessings because there's just so
much to count... those things are
the things... that make life
the best it can possibly be.

I don't know how I got so lucky
in my life, and I know I don't always
deserve it. But I want to thank you,
from the bottom of my heart, for
giving *so many* of those blessings and
beautiful things...
to me.

You Are
a Very
Special Person

I want you to know how amazing you are.
I want you to know how much you're
treasured and celebrated and quietly thanked.

I want you to feel really good...
    about who you are.
About all the great things you do!
I want you to appreciate your uniqueness.
Acknowledge your talents and abilities.
Realize what a beautiful soul you have.
Understand the wonder within...

You make so much sun shine through, and you inspire so much joy in the lives of everyone who is lucky enough to know you.

You are a very special person, giving so many people a reason to smile. You deserve to receive the best in return, and one of my heart's favorite hopes is that the happiness you give away will come back to warm you each and every day of your life.

———————⁐———————

I know your days are busy, but I hope they are giving back to you as much as you give to them.

And I know there are moments when things could be better, but I hope you'll remember that good things come to good people and that — without a doubt — you are one of the best.

There are so many wonderful things about you. But I think that the most admirable thing of all, at least to me, is that you do the things you do with an inner strength and a special kind of love. That's just the way you are.

You give life a gleam that most people only carry a glimpse of.

I've heard it said that

"You should never pass up a chance to let someone know how much they mean to you"...

There are so many moments in our lives when a little reminder and a few precious words would work wonders. I hope this is one of those times, because I want you to know how wonderful you are... to me.

There are days when I think of you — and of how important you are to my life — and I think to myself, "You know, I really should be sharing these precious feelings, and not keeping them all inside."

Why don't I share my thoughts more often? I guess that I keep waiting for the perfect time and place to tell you what I wish I could say...

Maybe it's just that I'd love to talk with you, face to smiling face, and be reassured by your acceptance and understanding before I venture out on a limb to say some of the things I keep in the deepest part of my heart.

But I'd like to start today by just saying thanks... for everything.
Thank you for being such a steady and joyful light in my life. Thank you for being a blessing I continue to count on through the years.

Thank you for brightening so many days and for doing it so beautifully.

———————⟊———————

I Think of You
Every Day

You probably don't realize how important you are to me. There are times when the one thing that helps me get through the day... is thinking of you.

You bring happiness to me when the world seems to be wearing a frown. When things don't quite go as planned and my world seems upside down, my thoughts of you help to set things right again.

You are so important to me. You make me think, you make me laugh, you make me feel alive. You put things in perspective for me. You provide support and encouragement, you lessen my worries, and you increase my joys. If my life were a puzzle, you would be the one piece that was a perfect fit.

Every day... I think of you.
And I've got a million smiles to prove it.

May You Always
Have an
Angel
by Your Side

May you always have an angel by your
side • Watching out for you in all the things
you do • Reminding you to keep believing
in brighter days • Finding ways for your
wishes and dreams to come true • Giving
you hope that is as certain as the sun •
Giving you the strength of serenity as your
guide • May you always have love and
comfort and courage •

And may you always have an angel by your
side • Someone there to catch you if you
fall • Encouraging your dreams • Inspiring
your happiness • Holding your hand and
helping you through it all •

In all of our days, our lives are always changing ◆ Tears come along as well as smiles ◆ Along the roads you travel, may the miles be a thousand times more lovely than lonely ◆ May they give you gifts that never, ever end: someone wonderful to love and a dear friend in whom you can confide ◆ May you have rainbows after every storm ◆ May you have hopes to keep you warm ◆

◆ And may you always have an angel by your side ◆

I think you're simply wonderful

If someone asked me to describe the kind of person who brings my heart the most happiness, I know exactly what I'd do. I'd gently describe some of the things I'm about to tell you...

I would begin by saying that I know one of the truly wonderful people of this world. I would tell them about this marvelous and amazing person who never fails to lift my spirits and who always puts things in perspective for me. I would tell them that my life is richer, my memories are more beautiful, and my serenity is more complete... all because I completely treasure you.

20 Beautiful Things
That Are True About You

You are something — and someone — very special.
You really are. No one else in this entire world is
exactly like you. You're a one-of-a-kind treasure,
uniquely here in this space and time. You are here
to shine in your own wonderful way, sharing your
smile in the best way you can, and remembering
all the while that a little light somewhere makes
a brighter light everywhere. You can — and you
do — make a wonderful contribution to this world,
and there are so many beautiful things about you.

You have qualities within you that many people
would love to have; and those who really and
truly know you are so glad that they do...

You have a big heart and a good and sensitive soul. You are gifted with thoughts and ways of seeing things that only special people know. You know that life doesn't always play by the rules, but that, in the long run, everything will work out. You understand that you and your actions are capable of turning anything around — and that joys once lost can always be found.

There is a resolve and an inner reserve of strength in you that few ever get to see. You have so many treasures within — those you're only beginning to discover, and all the ones you're already aware of.

Never forget what a treasure you are. That special person in the mirror may not always get to hear all the compliments you so sweetly deserve, but
     you are so worthy of
          such an abundance
               ...of friendship, joy, and love.

———————⌒———————

I just want
you to know
this

In the course of a person's lifetime,
there are so many prayers that get
whispered and so many hopes that
fill the heart. There are wishing stars
that spend their entire evenings
listening to all the things we long for.

I have said those prayers, and had
those hopes, and chatted with more
than my share of stars in the sky.

I always feel that if I ask and believe
and wish well enough, some things
are bound to turn out right.

But in all my prayers and wishes and
hopes, I couldn't have asked for
   a blessing
      more wonderful
         than you in my life.

For You

I don't know exactly what it is... but there is something very special about you.

It might be all the things I see on the surface: things that everyone notices and admires about you. Qualities and capabilities. Your wonderful smile, obviously connected to a warm and loving heart. It might be all the things that set you apart from everyone else.

Maybe it's the big things: the way you never hesitate to go miles out of your way to do what's right. The way your todays help set the stage for so many beautiful tomorrows. Or maybe it's the little things: words shared heart to heart. An unspoken understanding. Sharing seasons. Making some very wonderful memories. The joys of two people just being on the same page in each other's history...

If I could ever figure out all the magic that makes you so special, I'd probably find out that it's a combination of all these things — blended together with the best this world has to offer: friendship and love, dreams come true, strong feelings, gentle talks, listening, laughing, and simply knowing someone whose light shines brighter than any star.

You really are amazing.

And I feel very lucky to have been given
the gift of knowing
how special
you are.

When you read this

I want you to find a quiet place,
away from all the distractions
of the day; a favorite place
where you can just be by
yourself for a while...

a place where
you can close your eyes for
a few minutes to reminisce
    and happily imagine...

        the smiling face
        of someone who
        gets those smiles
        from thinking
        about
        you.

Carry the sun inside you, and reach out
for the dreams that guide you. You have
everything you need to take you where you
want to go. You have abilities and talents
and attributes that belong to you alone, and
you have what it takes to make your path of
success… lead to happiness.

You're a very special person.
You have qualities that get better every day!
You have the courage and strength to see
    things through.
You have smiles that will serve as your guides.
You have a light that will shine in you 'til the
    end of time…

You have known the truth of yesterday, and
you have an inner map that will lead the way
to a very beautiful tomorrow.
You have gifts that have never even been
opened and personal journeys waiting to be
explored. You have <u>so</u> <u>much</u> going for you.
You *are* a special person, and you have a
future that is in the best of hands. And you
need to remember: If you have plans you
want to act on and dreams you've always
wanted to come true...

You have what it takes, because...
            You
                have
                   you.

———————⌖———————

There will always be a special place in my heart...
for you.

It is a place that knows how very much there is
to appreciate about you. About your giving and
your sharing. About your beautiful spirit and
your kind and caring soul. About the generous
way you manage to brighten so many days.

It is a place that recognizes your uniqueness and
that celebrates the meaning of all this. It is a
place that inspires a more positive outlook on
everything every time I think of you.

Within my heart is a place that is filled with
warm and thankful feelings...
    feelings that understand
        how seldom
            someone like you comes along.

There Are
Only a Few
Really Special People

There are only a few people who are one of a kind. They are people who are gentle in spirit; who give with their hearts; who take things in stride; and who are truly beautiful inside.

There are only a few people who are completely unique. They are people who are not afraid to share whatever's on their mind; who are never anything but sincere; who are kind and giving; who make the days priceless; and who make my outlook on life more positive...

There are only a few people who possess
so many of these qualities that are seldom
found. It's nice to be around somebody
who understands; who shares their strength;
who makes the days together times to
remember; who provides with their very
presence the best of life and living — and
who helps me handle the rest of what life
is capable of giving.

There are only a few *really special* people...
and one of them is most definitely you.

———— ⮎ ————

Thanks to you, there are special feelings
inside of me that are absolutely invaluable
to my days and to my outlook on life.
I want you to know that there are times
when you are the only person who can
set the world right for me. I truly don't
know what I would ever do without you.

You are the one person who has never
let me down. You have changed more
frowns to smiles, and more concerns
into comforts, than anyone else I know.

I will always be thankful for...

The Special Connection
Between Us

As sure as the sun will rise in the sky —
you will always be a part of my life.
Whenever my days and my dreams
happen to find themselves on the same
page, and I have good news to report or
happy thoughts I want to share... I always
want to share them in a special way... with
you. And the same is true of any difficult
times: I know that the one person who can
remind me that the sun is still shining
above the clouds is the one person I am
so proud to know as well as I do.

And that person is you...

You are a <u>very</u> special part of my life.

You are a kind of "touchstone" for me.
You're a source of reflection, someone
whom I can talk with, listen to, or just
think of. And the next thing I know,
I see the way more clearly. I understand
myself a lot better. And I find myself
appreciating what a unique and wonderful
treasure you are... more and more as
time goes on.

I want you to know that there's
    one thing that will always be
        at the top of my list: And
            that is reminding you how
                thankful I am for this
                    special connection...
                        with you.

———————⟨⟩———————

You can make me laugh and live in the moment, you can make me reminisce of the past, and you give my tomorrows the happy hope that all of this is going to last... forever.

If someone asked me to describe the best kind of person, I'd tell them that it is someone with a very special soul. Someone you feel an affinity for right from the start, a person with whom you have a bond that lasts through time, sharing more sunshine than words could ever begin to say. I'd tell them to find someone exactly like you... and then to simply hold on to the countless joys that will come their way.

Remember that you can always count on me

When life isn't easy and you wonder if anyone understands what you're going through, I want you... to reach out to me. Even if we find ourselves miles apart, don't ever forget that my heart is filled with so many hopes for your happiness.

I want you to feel like you can tell me everything that's on your mind. I want to be able to help you find a lot more smiles and make your days more joyful and filled with all the serenity you so dearly deserve...

When you wonder if there is anyone who
cares completely and unconditionally, look
my way. Let down your guard, and know
that it's okay to bare your soul with someone
who knows you as well as I do. When you
need to talk things out, realize that you'll
find a very loving listener... in me.

It doesn't matter what it's for; if it's important
to you, then it's important to me. What
matters most is that you gently remember:
Sometimes two heads (and two hearts)
are better than one can be, and you
can always count on me to be
there for you.

———————— ⌒ ————————

We have a bond that
   will always be there for us.

No matter where we go
   or how much time passes,
   you and I will always,
   in a very special way,
   remain together in spirit.
And that knowledge is
   cherished by me as the one
   thing that must never change.

In a world of constant transition,
   I pray that what we feel
      toward one another
         will *always* stay the same.

Thank you for the way
you touch
my life

Thank you for the
way you touch my life.

With understanding and joy.
With simplicity and peace.
With hope.
With precious knowledge.
With every single thing
    that is sweetly shared between us.

Thank you for all the warmth.
The listening that goes deeper
    than hearing my spoken words.
Thank you for gentle advice and for
    sharing smile-making remedies that
    can cure any case of the blues.
Thank you for bringing
    the morning light
    shining bright and
    beautifully back to me
        every time
            I thought it was gone...

Thank you for never being
gone too long from my sight.
For truly, absolutely inspiring me.
For giving me enough leeway to
be a little crazy without ever
holding it against me.
For letting me know that the bridge
that exists between us will rise
above whatever comes along.

Thank you for the riches untold
and the reassurance of letting
my soul feel so at home.
Thank you for every memory
and each little moment
you have given me.
Thank you for letting me know
how strong and sure and steady
unconditional caring
can really be.

Special People

The special people in this world are the most precious and the most appreciated people of all. No matter what happens, they always understand. They go a million miles out of their way. They hold your hand.

They bring you smiles, when a smile is exactly what you need. They listen, and they hear what is said in the spaces between the words. They care, and they let you know you're in their prayers.

Special people always know the perfect thing to do. They can make your whole day just by saying something that no one else could have said. Sometimes you feel like they share with you a secret language that others can't tune in to...

Special people can guide you, inspire you, comfort you, and light up your life with laughter. Special people understand your moods and nurture your needs, and they lovingly know just what you're after.

When your feelings come from deep inside and they need to be spoken to someone you don't have to hide from, you share them... with special people. When good news comes, special people are the first ones you turn to. And when feelings overflow and tears need to fall, special people help you through it all.

Special people bring sunlight into your life. They warm your world with their presence, whether they are far away or close by your side.

Special people are gifts
    that bring such happiness,
and they're treasures
    that money can't buy.

———————⌒———————

To One Very Wonderful Person

It seems like there are so many times when my heart is filled to the brim with all the special thoughts I have... of one very wonderful person.

I turn to that one source of joy, comfort, and companionship so naturally... because that's where my heart and soul want to be. I think that's how bonds are formed and how closeness grows: two lives begin to overlap and share a special place together. And the more they do that, the more they know that their shared space has a kind of sacred quality to it.

It's a place where everything is always okay. Where it's nurturing and safe and supportive. It's a place where we're free to be exactly who we are, without all the worries of acting dumb or saying the wrong thing. It's a place where we can bring our concerns and hopes and dreams out into the open...

It's a place where there are beautiful bridges instead of all the walls that separate so many other people. It's a very privileged place to be, and I feel very lucky to hold the key. There's only one other person who has the duplicate to it — and who always knows where that sanctuary is.

There are so many moments in my life when only THE most special person of all is the one I turn to. I truly don't know what I would ever do without that person, that kind of caring, and that inspiring place in my life. It means the world to me to have those smiling eyes, those shared memories, and that understanding heart to turn to. All because of this very special someone, I have known so many blessings I never want to be without. I'll give you three guesses who that someone might be...

but the first two don't count.

———————⟨——————

Some People Are
So Wonderful

Some people seem like they have the
warmth of the morning sun in their spirits
and more gentleness in their hearts than
words can describe.

Some people are so remarkable and rare;
so filled with precious qualities. They are
the ones who are absolute jewels, sparkling
with such a special presence...

They're the ones who are invaluable to a
world that needs more wishes to come true...
and more exceptional people to look up to...

Some people have an amazing way of touching
the hearts of others, in a time and a place
where the nicest feelings and the deepest
gratitude all come together. There's such a
special appreciation for them, but the thanks
they deserve is often long overdue.

Some people will be treasured forever.

And one of those people...
is you.

Always Stay as Special as You Are

I wish you knew how much you mean to me.
I wish I could describe the thankful, joyful
feelings I have inside of me.
All because of you. I think that...
in the same way that the brightest stars
are always shining in the sky,
the most wonderful people in our lives
    take up a special place in our hearts
        and remain with us forever.

You are one of those ever-present,
perfect feelings that always feels so much
    at home in my heart.

Because I know you, I know that there
are people who really are everything
that the word "special" could ever mean...

It may be because special people are so kind, so understanding, so remarkable and rare. It may be because they are so good at inspiring smiles. It may be because special people have the power to make good times into truly great days, and in difficult times they see you through and keep you on a path that leads right back to all the blessings in your life.

I am so thankful that the joys and feelings you inspire... came into my life and that they will live on and brighten so many moments in my heart's memory. I will always think of them as beautiful gifts.

And I'll never forget who gave them to me.

I am beginning to understand
how important it is to let the
people I care about the most...
   know how much I care.

I could try to thank *you* for
the rest of my days, but even
then, I don't know if I'd be able
to convey everything my heart
would like to say. But I hope
you'll always remember this...

You are the kind of person
   everyone would
      love to have
         in their lives.

24 Things
to Always Remember...
and One Thing
to Never Forget

Your presence is a present to the world.
You're unique and one of a kind.
Your life can be what you want it to be.
Take the days just one at a time.

Count your blessings, not your troubles.
You'll make it through
    whatever comes along.
Within you are so many answers.
Understand, have courage, be strong.

Don't put limits on yourself.
So many dreams are waiting to be realized.
Decisions are too important
    to leave to chance.
Reach for your peak, your goal, your prize...

Nothing wastes more energy than worrying.
The longer one carries a problem,
    the heavier it gets.
Don't take things too seriously.
Live a life of serenity, not a life of regrets.

Remember that a little love
    goes a long way.
Remember that a lot... goes forever.
Remember that friendship
    is a wise investment.
Life's treasures are people... together.

Realize that it's never too late.
Do ordinary things in an extraordinary way.
Have health and hope and happiness.
Take the time to wish upon a star.

And don't ever forget...
    for even a day... how very special you are.

———————⌢———————

If I could have
a wish come true...

I would wish for
nothing but wonderful things
    to come
       to you.

In your life, which is
    so precious to me,
may troubles, worries, and problems
never linger; may they only make you
that much stronger and able and wise.

And may you rise each day with sunlight
in your heart, success in your path,
answers to your prayers,
    and that smile
       — that I love to see —
         always there... in your eyes.

About the Author

Douglas Pagels has been a favorite Blue Mountain Arts® writer for many years. His philosophical sayings and sentiments on friendship and love have been translated into seven languages and shared with millions of people worldwide in notecards, calendars, and his previous books. He lives in the mountains of Colorado with his wife and two sons.